The Smallest House Cook Book

Margaret Williams

Text © Margaret Williams 1992

Copyright © by Gwasg Carreg Gwalch 1992.
All rights reserved. No part of this publication
may be reproduced or transmitted, in any form
or by any means, without permission.

ISBN: 0-86381-223-6

Cover: Old photograph of the Smallest House

First published in 1992 by Gwasg Carreg Gwalch,
Capel Garmon, Llanrwst, Gwynedd, Wales.

Tel: 0690 710261

Printed in Wales.

Contents:

Introduction

The Smallest House in the countries of Britain on the quayside at Conwy which measures 72″ across and 122″ high, was built in the 16th century and lived in until 1900. The last inhabitant was a fisherman named Robert Jones who was 6′3″ tall. Before him an elderly couple lived there. In 1900 the house was condemned for human habitation but the editor of the local paper persuaded the owner, also called Robert Jones, to tour the country measuring small houses to prove this was the smallest. This he did and the house became a showplace and was subsequently mentioned in the Guinness Book of Records. The house is still owned by the same family and this book is written by one of the great grand-daughters.

After learning that Robert Jones, the last inhabitant, lived in the Smallest House for 15 years, the reaction of most people is "Where did he cook?"

On the fire, they are told. And, indeed, he must surely go down in history as the man who made the most of his surroundings. Unable to stand upright in the downstairs room which served as living quarters, kitchen and bathroom, he cooked on the tiny fireplace and baked in the incredibly small oven, having harvested most of his food from the sea.

Robert Jones's basic recipes were simple but he was able to enjoy such delicacies as mussels, salmon and mullet. Here his dishes have been adapted for modern cooking methods. I hope you enjoy them as much as he did!

Fishing at Conwy

Where the Conwy river meets the Irish sea has always been a fruitful place for fishermen all through the ages. The Romans came and stated that they saw men fishing from coracles on the Conwy river pools, and at the estuary they themselves found that shell-fish and even pearls were plentiful. Today, as ever, the mussel fishermen are still an important part of Conwy's character.

Netting salmon and sea trout is allowed to certain families in the tidal waters and, of course, the unique fish of the Conwy river — *brwyniad* (the sparling) — is also caught here in season. When Conwy developed as a harbour, fishing vessels went out to search the Irish Sea for plaice, mackerel, mullet and herring.

Conwy quay still holds its own as a fisherman's quay. Walk along the front at high tide when the fishing boats arrive home; watch the unloading, see the ropes being drawn into coils, the nets hung out, the lobster pots and fish boxes piled on the quayside. Buy your fresh fish here and go home with your lungs full of salty air, knowing that the fishing industry is alive and well in Conwy.

Spring

While prancing lambs and nodding daffodils are regarded as the harbingers of spring in most places, in Conwy it is an unusual fish which spells the start of the new season.

For sparlings are caught in only two rivers in the British Isles — here and one in Scotland. They arrive in January and February, spawn in March or April and then depart.

They are tiny, of a beautiful form and colour with transparent heads and their skin is thin and fine. Their peculiar scent is often compared with cucumber or violet but those who speak Welsh liken it to rushes, hence the name *Brwyniad*.

Regarded as a Welsh delicacy, these little fish owe their existence to an Irish saint.

Centuries ago, two holy women of Ireland, Modwenna and Bride, were sitting in a meadow near the shore of their homeland along with two of their servants when suddenly they found themselves at sea. The piece of land they were sitting on had broken away from the Irish mainland and they floated for a day and a night until their island landed on the shores of Britain, at the mouth of the river Conwy.

This piece of Ireland became part of our coastline and is where Deganwy now stands. Bride settled here and became known as Ffraid and is commemorated in the village of Llansanffraid (Glan Conwy) while Modwenna left and went to live in Mercia. There she became St Modwenna of the Forest of Arden and it was she who wrote of their incredible journey to Wales.

St Ffraid had been here but a short time when there was a dire famine in the land and so serious did it become that there was not even enough fish in the river to allay the great hunger of the people.

In desperation they sought her out and asked her to pray for their plight but she did more than that — she went down to the river and gathered a quantity of rushes which she threw into the water. And as soon as they touched the surface they turned into fully grown fish.

There was enough for everyone and more beside and people said they tasted of the rushes from which they were formed. So they called them *Brwyniad* and regarded them as one of life's most wonderful gifts.

Because it is traditionally a Conwy fish, the sparling plays an important part in an old custom. Whenever the Marquis of Hertford passes through the town he is entitled to ask for a dish of sparling — this was one of the conditions laid down after one of his ancestors, Viscount Conwy of Kilultagh, bought the castle for £100 from King Charles I, to whom he had been Secretary of State.

Subsequently the castle was handed over to the town but the tradition is still maintained — the last time was in August 1958 when the Marquis and Marchioness of Hertford visited the castle and were presented with a salmon by the Mayor and Constable (Mr O. M. Roberts) as sparlings were out of season.

Sparlings

Sparlings make a delicious luncheon or breakfast dish and are especially recommended for invalids.

To Bake:
12 sparlings
breadcrumbs
2 oz butter
salt and cayenne to taste
parsley
lemon

Method:
Wash and dry the fish thoroughly and arrange in a greased baking dish. Cover with fine breadcrumbs and place little pieces of butter over them. Season and bake for about 15 minutes at 375°F, 190°C, Mark 5. Just before serving add a squeeze of lemon juice and garnish with fried parsley and a slice of lemon.

To Fry:
12 sparlings
egg
breadcrumbs
a little flour

Method:
Wash fish, flour lightly, dip in beaten egg, cover with fine breadcrumbs and fry in oil. Drain and serve with melted butter.

Each recipe is sufficient for four persons.

Plaice

Conwy plaice is renowned for its flavour and is delicious grilled on the bone or filleted. But for a change, try baking it.

Baked Plaice:
8 fillets plaice
2 oz sliced mushrooms
small onion, skinned and finely chopped
6 tbsp milk
1 level tbspn cornflour
squeeze of lemon juice
salt and pepper
parsley to garnish

Method:
Grease an ovenproof dish. Fold each fillet with both ends underneath and place in the dish. Squeeze some lemon juice over and season with salt and pepper. Sprinkle the mushrooms and onion on top and add the milk. Bake at 375°F, 190°C, Mark 5 for 15-20 minutes. Blend the cornflour with the remaining liquid from the fish and put in a saucepan. Bring to the boil and cook for one minute. Pour over fillets and garnish with parsley. Serves 4.

Kippers

Poached:
Put kippers into a frying pan, cover with boiling water and poach gently for about 5 minutes or until tender. Drain and serve with a knob of butter.

Grilled:
Dot the kippers with butter and grill gently for 4-5 minutes each side.

Baked:
Wrap kippers in foil and place in oven 375°F, 190°C, Mark 5. Serve with a knob of butter.

Anglesey Eggs

This old Welsh recipe for a filling luncheon or supper dish when meat was scarce has now found its way to the menus of smart restaurants as a first course, and very popular it is, too.

You need:
6 medium-sized leeks
2 tbspns butter
2 oz grated cheese plus 2 tbspns grated cheese
8 hard-boiled eggs
1 lb hot mashed potato
salt and pepper
1 tbspn flour
½ pint warm milk

Method:
Clean the leeks and chop into pieces and cook in boiling salted water for 10 mintues. Strain well and add to the hot mashed potato. Add half the butter, season to taste and beat until fluffy. Arrange around the edge of a fireproof dish and keep warm. Heat the other tbspn butter, stir in the flour and add the warmed milk, stirring well. Put in the 2 oz grated cheese and mix well. Cut up the eggs, and put in the middle of the leek and potatoes and cover with the cheese sauce. Sprinkle the remaining cheese on top and put into a hot oven 400°F, 200°C, Mark 6 until the top is golden brown. Serves 4.

Pancakes

Traditionally served during the last feast before Lent, pancakes used up the eggs and butter which were not eaten once fasting started on Ash Wednesday.

Basic Recipe:
1 egg
4 oz flour
lard
¼ tspn salt
½ pint milk

Method:
Sieve flour and salt into a bowl. Make a well in the centre, drop in the egg and gradually add the milk then mix to a smooth batter. Beat well for about 5 minutes. Melt a knob of lard in a frying pan and when smoking hot pour in enough batter to cover the base of the pan and cook gently for 1-2 minutes. When golden brown turn over and cook the other side. Serve with sugar and lemon juice or jam.

Alternative Fillings:
Grated cheese, sliced cooked mushrooms, diced ham or bacon, cooked flaked fish or shellfish.

Plate Cake

You need:
8 oz flour
4 oz butter or margarine
4 oz sugar
4 oz dried fruit
2 eggs
¼ pint milk
1 heaped tspn baking powder
½ tspn grated nutmeg

Method:
Rub fat into flour. Add sugar, fruit, baking powder and nutmeg. Mix in beaten eggs and gradually add milk to make a fairly soft mixture. Turn onto a well greased 9″ oven plate and spread evenly. Cook in moderate oven, 350°F, 180°C, Mark 4 for 20 minutes, then reduce heat to 300°F, 150°C, Mark 2 for a further 35 minutes. The cake should be lightly browned and firm to touch. Turn out on wire rack to cool.

Summer

Summer brings an abundance of fish to the river — fat salmon caught in the upper reaches, shoals of mackerel, mullet and herrings.

Like other fishermen Robert Jones sold his catches to the hotels that were springing up on the coastline for the railway was bringing in the first trickle of tourists, but he invariably kept some fish for himself which he enjoyed on the long, light evenings, eating at his small circular table and looking out at the animated river scene.

The forebears of Robert Jones were taught how to fish by the monks of the Cistercian abbey at Conwy. The fact that this was a lonely place is borne out by the decision of the Cistercian Order to build their house here in the 12 century for they always chose to live far from the haunts of men.

Llywelyn the Great endowed the abbey with a great extent of land and gave the monks many privileges and immunities, including any ship wrecked on their territory. The monastery had extensive fisheries on the river and also at Llandrillo-yn-Rhos where a weir still exists. Nearby is a small cell with a well, or spring, where a monk is said to have prayed daily for the success of the fishing.

After the conquest in 1284, Edward I of England thought the monks would enjoy a more peaceful life in the Conwy Valley than in the garrison town that was taking shape all around them, so he removed the abbey to Maenan, about 10 miles up the river, and that is where the community continued until the Dissolution of the Monasteries.

Salmon has been caught in the river Conwy every summer since those far-off days. The season starts on April 1 and ends on August 31. Three fishing families have their own traditional stretches of river — the Joneses (descendants of Robert Jones, the owner of the Smallest House) at Tal-y-cafn, the Hugheses (who can trace their line back 400 years) below Baclaw and the Cravens (comparative newcomers who arrived from Lancashire in the last century) at Caerhun.

Salmon

Cooking salmon should be kept simple. You can bake a whole fish after spreading with butter and lemon and wrapping in double foil — in a moderate oven 350°F, 180°C, Mark 4 — for 15 minutes to the pound or poach in boiling salted water with a dash of vinegar or lemon juice for the same length of time.

Small steaks should be poached or grilled. If grilling, brush with oil.

Welsh Plated Salmon:
Place steaks in fireproof soup plates, add 2 tbspns milk, cover and stand on top of pans of boiling water in which new potatoes and asparagus can be cooking. All this takes about 20 minutes. Eat it from the plates with vegetable accompaniments and a tossed salad.

Poached Salmon Steaks:
4 salmon steaks, 2-3 ounces melted butter, parsley sprigs and lemon wedges.

Court Bouillon:
½ pint water or dry white wine
rind and juice of ½ lemon
1 bay leaf
2 peppercorns
1 sprig parsley
½ tspn salt
1 small onion, sliced

Method:
Arrange the steaks in a large shallow frying pan. Add the ingredients for court bouillon. Cover with foil and the lid. Bring slowly to the boil. Remove pan from heat, take off lid and leave fish in cooking liquid for about a minute. Drain and place in serving dish. Pour melted butter over.

Mackerel

So much mackerel is caught in the river Conwy in summer that one is constantly seeking different ways of cooking these tasty fish. One golden rule — remember they are at their best cooked the day they are caught.

Grilled Mackerel:
Slit fish down the back, season and brush with oil before grilling.

Baked Mackerel:
4 mackerel
1 5fl oz carton natural yoghurt
4 tbspns fresh double cream
salt and pepper
lemon wedges
watercress

Method:
Preheat oven, 375°F, 190°C, Mark 5. Wash fish, dry and place in an ovenproof dish. Beat the yoghurt and the cream together, season and pour over fish. Bake for 15-20 minutes. Serve garnished with lemon wedges and watercress.

Stuffed Mackerel:
2 mackerel, split and boned
1½ oz butter
1 oz fresh breadcrumbs
1½ level tbspns watercress (chopped)
salt and pepper

Method:
Lay the fish in a lightly greased ovenproof dish. Cream the butter until soft, add breadcrumbs and watercress, season and mix well together. Put half the mixture into each mackerel, cover the dish and bake at 375°F, 190°C, Mark 5 for 30-35 minutes. Serve with wedges of lemon and garnish with sprigs of watercress.

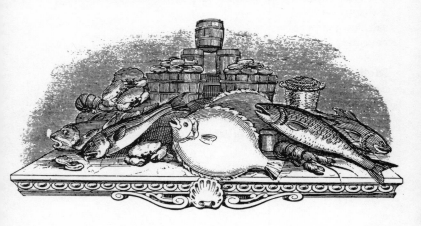

Mullet

If you have not cleaned mullet before then get someone else to do it, preferably one who is used to gutting fish as this can be most off-putting to a novice.

Small Mullet:
Place in hot water and cook gently for about 15-20 minutes. Serve with anchovy or melted butter sauce.

Large Mullet:
Cut into steaks and grill gently. Serve with chipped or mashed potatoes and a green vegetable salad.

Crab

Dressed Crab:
1 medium-sized crab
1 hard-boiled egg
2 tbspns vinegar
1 tbspns oil
salt and pepper,
cayenne

Method:
Scoop meat from the shells and mix with the vinegar and oil.
Season well. Clean the largest of the shells, put in the mixture. Rub
the egg yolk through a sieve and chop the white, then use for
garnish along with slices of lemon, parsley and egg.

Lamb

From the scattered farms around Conwy would come fresh meat in exchange for fish and one of the most tasty was lamb, a treat for Sunday dinner.

Roast Breast of Lamb:
1 breast of lamb with bones taken out
salt and pepper
3 oz fresh breadcrumbs
1 level tbspn parsley, chopped
grated rind of ½ a lemon
1 oz melted butter
1 standard egg

Method:
Place lamb skin-side down and season with salt and pepper. Mix together the breadcrumbs, parsley, lemon rind and butter and bind with the beaten egg. Spread the stuffing on the inside of the lamb, roll up and secure with string.
Roast at 375°F, 190°C, Mark 5 for about 1½ hours. Serve with roast or boiled potatoes and vegetables.

Autumn

When the leaves turning to a rich gold reflected their glorious patterns on the river Robert Jones put aside his nets and prepared for the long winter ahead. But before the cold weather set in there was a time of respite when fisherfolk took their catches to church where they were placed alongside the fruits of the earth at the harvest festival service and then came the Honey Fair with stalls set up in the streets and trading and bartering going on well into the night by the light of lanterns.

Last century writer Canon Robert Williams said the superiority of the flavour of Conwy honey was probably due to its being extracted from the heath blossoms and other wild flowers on the neighbouring mountains. The average price in 1835 was two shillings a quart or eightpence a pound.

Conwy was famous for its honey from early times, something that is borne out by an item in an expense list of Edward 1 at Rhuddlan Castle: "Repairing a cart of the King's, conveying a pipe of honey from Aberconwy to Rothelan, 1s 4d."

The Honey Fair on September 13 and the Seed Fair on March 26 are the only survivors for before the First World War there were ten fairs every year in Conwy. They were opened by members of the Corporation who "proceeded with their wands to the top of the street and read the proclamation."

Then the Mayor, Alderman and Baliffs would, in the King's name, command every man coming to the fair to keep the peace and not bear any manner of weapons or harness upon him under pain of imprisonment.

After the Honey Fair the weather usually deteriorated and the cold autumn winds drove people indoors where they whiled away the evenings telling one another stories of the past, and when the gales howled outside it was time to remember the mermaid and her curse.

For it was on a rough day that a mermaid floated in on a high tide and as she lay wretchedly on the shore she asked some fishermen to throw her back into the sea. They refused, for the sea had taken much from them and they were unwilling to help one of its creatures. As she tried to slide across the stones to reach the water's edge they laughed and jested at the spectacle she made, but when the tide rose and she was carried away on the crest of a wave their faces fell. For she cursed the town and its inhabitants for evermore.

Some people still refer to the mermaid's words when ill fortune strikes. And there are many who swear they hear her plaintive wail growing fainter and fainter as a ghostly wave carries her to the open sea . . .

Honey

The profusion of honey at the fair would tempt Robert Jones to stock up for winter, for one can use this versatile product in many different ways:

* Make a sauce with warm honey, add a dash of sherry and pour over a sponge pudding.
* Spread honey on hot, buttered cinnamon toast.
* Mix with butter and raisins to make a delicious filling for baked apples.

Honey Pork:
2½ lb loin pork
12 oz strained honey
3 tbspns prepared mustard
salt and pepper

Method:
Bone and roll the loin — or ask the butcher to do it for you — and salt and pepper the inside beforehand. Mix the strained honey and mustard. Sprinkle the meat with salt and pepper. Coat all the sides with the honey and mustard mixture, using a palette knife. Wrap in tin foil. Place in a rack in a baking pan and then put into pre-heated oven — 400°F, 200°C, Mark 6 — and bake for at least two hours. For the last 20 minutes of baking, unfold the tin foil so the roast can brown. Test with a skewer to make sure it is done. Eat cold.

Honey Mousse:
6 egg yolks
1 lb strained dark honey
3 egg whites
16 oz double cream

Method:
Beat the yolks of eggs and then beat in 1 lb strained honey. Put in a double boiler over hot, not boiling, water. Stirring constantly, cook until it thickens. Chill. Beat three egg whites stiff and fold into the honey mixture. Whip the double cream and fold in. Pack in a mould and store in the freezing compartment.

Bara Brith

This would be made in the autumn and stored until Christmas. In the old days it was a substitute for cake which many people could not afford, but is now regarded as a teatime delicacy.

Remember — keep everything warm!

You need:
1 lb wheatmeal flour
1 tspn yeast
2 oz brown molasses sugar
3 oz butter
¼ pint milk
3 oz seedless raisins
3 oz currants
1 oz candied peel
1 tspn salt
1 tspn mixed spice

Method:
Cut and melt the butter into the ¼ pint milk. Cream the yeast with a little of the warm milk, then add to the flour and salt, which should also be warm. Work into a dough with the warm milk. Set to rise until doubled in bulk. This should take about an hour. Now knock the dough back to its original size before the second kneading, during which the sugar, spices and fruit should be worked in. Put into a warmed and buttered 3 pint loaf tin, leave to rise to top of tin. This will take about 40 minutes.
Bake 20-30 minutes in the centre of a hot oven — 400°F, 200°C, Mark 6 — covering the top with paper or foil for the last 10 minutes. Leave to cool before turning out. Brush top with sugar syrup to glaze.

Leek Pie

You need:
10 large leeks
1 tbspn butter
4 rashers chopped bacon or ham
2 eggs, beaten, mixed with ½ pint cream or milk
salt and pepper
pastry — use the frozen variety for quickness

Method:
Roll out pastry and line a 8″ flan tin. Wash the leeks and chop into
1″ pieces. Heat the butter then toss the leeks into it until they
soften. Do not allow them to brown. Spread onto the pastry, add
the bacon or ham and season. Beat the eggs with the cream or milk
and pour over leeks, then cook in a moderate oven — 350°F,
180°C, Mark 4 — for about 35 minutes until the mixture is set and
slightly golden. Eat hot or cold. Serves 4.

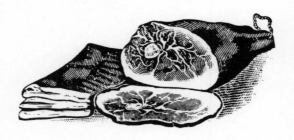

Welsh Herrings

You need:
6 herrings, filleted
1 large cooking apple
2 large potatoes
1 large onion
1 oz butter or margarine
1 tspn sage
salt and pepper

Method:
Peel and slice potatoes, apple and onion. Line a greased ovenproof dish with half the potatoes and place onto a layer of apples and then of onion. Lay out the herrings, sprinkle with salt and pepper and then roll up, place on onion and sprinkle with sage. Cover with remaining sliced potatoes. Half fill dish with boiling water. Put small pieces of butter on top. Cover and bake at 350°F, 180°C, Mark 4 for 45 minutes. Remove cover and brown the top for about half an hour. Serves 4-6.

Pwdin Mynwy

You need:

12 oz white breadcrumbs
2 oz granulated sugar
vanilla essence
2 oz butter
¼ pint milk
4 tbspns raspberry jam
3 egg whites
2 oz caster sugar

Method:

Boil the milk and pour over the breadcrumbs. Soak for 5 minutes. Stir in melted butter and add granulated sugar. Spread half the jam in the bottom of a greased round ovenproof dish. Pour in mixture, cover with rest of jam. Beat egg whites until stiff. Fold in caster sugar. Pile on top of jam. Cook for about 30 minutes at 350°F, 180°C, Mark 4, until golden brown.

Winter

For Robert Jones and his fellow fishermen, winter was a most gruelling time for this was when they rowed their small boats to the estuary in all manner of weather and there they gathered the blue-shelled mussels, a tradition still carried on by their descendants today, although the journey to and from the beds is now made by motor launch.

Mussel gathering is indeed Conwy's oldest industry and dates back to the Roman Conquest. It is said that the Roman camp at Caerhun, a few miles up the river, was chosen because of its proximity to the pearls which were to be found in the mussels at Conwy. And Julius Caesar dedicated a breastplate to Venus Genitrix, covered with British pearls, which was placed in her temple in Rome.

Pearls are obtained from two kinds of mussels, the *Mya Margaritifera* and the *Mytikus Edulis*. The former are obtained higher up the river, above Trefriw, and it was a pearl from this species which Sir Richard Wynne of Gwydir, chamberlain to Catherine, consort of Charles II, presented to Her Majesty and which is now in the Crown Jewels.

The other variety is found in abundance at the mouth of the river and in the old days the men, women and children who gathered them at ebb tide took them to a pearl kitchen on the Morfa, a small room, about five feet square and six to seven feet high, constructed of wattle and gorse with a hole in the roof for the smoke to escape.

Here the mussels were boiled in a large iron pot on a fire. They were then picked out and put into a tub and crushed by bare-footed children. When water was added the animal matter floated and this was fed to ducks. The sediment, when dried, was separated by a goose-wing and the pearls were put into little bags and taken to Chester where they were sold from six to 12 shillings an ounce.

In 1834 as much as £300 to £400 a year was being paid for pearls and 40 people were employed at the fishery which produced an average of about 160 oz a week. The pearls were said to be equal to those found in any part of the British Isles.

Pearls are occasionally found in the shells of mussels which are gathered from September until the end of March although they are incredibly small ones.

The musselmen lead a hard life, often going out on the tide in the early hours of the morning and gathering with long-handled rakes, the method that has been used for centuries. Not that their task ends there, for after landing their catches they have the arduous task of removing the debris from the shells before the mussels are taken to the Ministry of Agriculture and Fisheries purification tanks in the shadow of the castle where they go through a 48 hour process before being sent to market.

Fresh Fish

Moules Mariniere

Wash the mussels in cold running water. Throw away any with open shells. For four quarts of mussels, melt four tbspns butter in a large heavy frying pan, stir in two small, peeled, sliced onions. Add the mussels, sprinkle with 1 tbspn flour, 3 tbspns water, cover and shake the pan over the heat for five minutes. Stir the mussels, cook for another minute until the shells open and the liquid comes out. Remove beards from mussels. Put cooked mussels in a hot tureen and strain the stock in the pan through a fine sieve. Serve sprinkled with chopped parsley. Eat with hunks of crusty bread.

Moules Mariniere are best eaten from soup plates. Robert Jones would have used a spoon for the gravy and eaten the mussels with a pair of empty shells — they still do this in France.

Don't forget to have extra dishes for the discarded empty shells.

Lobscaws

This was one of the mainstays of winter — a nourishing, hot meal eaten with relish after a morning at the mussel beds. Old fashioned cooks believed the best way of making it was to start the day before it was needed — in this way fat could be skimmed off and the flavours given a chance to blend together.

You need:
2-3 lb best end neck cutlets
1 large sliced onion
3 leeks
2 medium sliced carrots
1 medium parsnip
1 small swede or 2 white turnips
2 tbspns chopped parsley
6 small potatoes
salt and pepper
4 pints water

Method:
Trim the meat of fat, cover with cold water, add salt and pepper and bring to the boil. Simmer slowly for 1 hour then leave to get cold and skim off all the fat. Put in all the vegetables except 1 leek, the potatoes and half the parsley, cover and simmer very slowly for 1 hour, then add the potatoes cut in half and continue for 20 minutes. Add the remainder of the parsley and finely chop the remaining leek on top. Cook for 5 minutes and serve.

Welsh Chicken Pie

Chicken was a rare treat, and the favourite way of serving it was in a pie to be eaten on Christmas Day, the remainder served cold on Boxing Day.

You need:
½ lb shortcrust pastry
1 boiled chicken, jointed and boned
4 slices ham
1 cup cooked leeks OR 1 cup chopped parsley
1 small onion, finely chopped
pinch mace
¾ pint jellied stock

Method:
Keep the stock from the boiled chicken. Make sure the pastry is kept in a cool place while you are preparing the filling.

Put leeks or parsley into a deep pie dish, then add a layer of ham and the chicken pieces, onion and mace. Pour on chicken stock. Roll out pastry on floured board and cover pie dish, pressing edges well down. Cut slit in the top and brush lightly over with milk. Bake at 375°F, 190°C, Mark 5 for about 40 minutes until golden brown. Eat hot or cold. Serves 6.

Stock:
Like all good householders in the last century Robert Jones would have had his stockpot. Into this went the bones from the chicken he made into a pie, giblets, chopped onion, chopped carrots, chopped celery. These days we can add bouquet garni to enhance the flavour.

Method:
All these ingredients should be put into the stockpot and covered with water then simmered for 5-6 hours. Afterwards, strain the stock and remove fat when cold. The stock can be used instead of water to enrich soups, stews and gravies.

Fish Soup

Robert Jones certainly made the most of the fish he caught. Even a cod's head did not go to waste as we can see from this recipe.

You need:
1 cod's head
2 pints water
1 small carrot
¼ turnip
½ onion
1 stalk celery
bouquet garni
salt and pepper
½ pint white sauce
chopped parsley

Method:
Make sure you wash the cod's head thoroughly before putting it in the water. Bring slowly to the boil and skim well. Prepare and chop vegetables, add bouquet garni and salt and simmer for about 1 hour then strain. Remove flesh from cod's head and cut into pieces. Make sauce and blend with the stock. Season, then add the fish and parsley.

Fish Pie

You need:
½ lb cooked fish
1 lb cooked potatoes, mashed (or use instant packet if pushed for time)
1 tspn chopped parsley
½ pint white sauce
1 hard-boiled egg
seasoning

Method:
Remove skin and bone from fish. Mash potatoes and season. Flake fish, add sauce, seasoning and parsley, then the sliced egg and turn into a greased pie dish. Cover with mashed potatoes. Brush with egg or milk. Bake in hot oven, 425°F, 220°C, Mark 7, for about 15 minutes. Brown top under grill. Serves 4-5.

Bread and Butter Pudding

You need:
4 slices bread and butter
1 egg
1 oz sugar
2 oz currants and sultanas
1 pint milk
pinch of salt
nutmeg

Method:
Cut the bread and butter into strips and place in a buttered pie dish. Sprinkle each layer with sugar and fruit. Add salt to the milk, heat it and pour onto the beaten egg. Strain into pie dish, grate nutmeg on top and leave to soak for ½ hour. Bake in a moderate oven 350°F, 180°C, Mark 4, for ½ hour until golden brown and set.

All Seasons

Sometimes Robert Jones would give himself a treat — cakes which he could take with him when he went fishing, a Welsh rarebit for a mid-day repast, even some treacle toffee for high days and holidays . . .

Welsh Cakes

You need:
12 oz plain flour
8 oz butter or margarine
5 oz currants and sultanas
1 heaped tspn baking powder
pinch of salt
½ tspn mixed spice
1 egg
milk

Method:
Sieve flour, baking powder and salt together and rub in fat. Add sugar, fruit and spice. Mix in beaten egg and enough milk to make a stiff dough. Roll out to ½ inch thickness on floured board and cut into 3 inch rounds. Cook on a lightly greased griddle on a moderate heat for 4 minutes each side. Check cakes are cooked through. Sprinkle with sugar on cooking tray.

Welsh Rarebit

You need:
8 oz grated cheese
2 tspns flour
1 oz butter
2 tspns Worcestershire sauce
1 level tspn dried mustard
4 tbspns milk
pepper
4 slices bread

Method:
Melt butter in saucepan, add cheese, flour, sauce, mustard and pepper. Stir in milk gradually over gentle heat until all is melted into a thick paste. Toast 4 slices of bread on one side only. Spread mixture over untoasted side and pop under hot grill to brown.

Treacle Toffee

You need:
8 oz butter
8 oz treacle
12 oz demerara sugar
¾ gill water
a good pinch cream of tartar

Method:
Using a large pan, dissolve all the ingredients except cream of tartar which you add when it comes to the boil. Boil gently for about 20 minutes or until a little dropped into cold water sets. Stir occasionally. Pour into oiled tin.

Mincemeat

You need:
4 oz raisins
4 oz currants
4 oz peeled apple
4 oz raw sugar
2 oz sultanas
grated rind and juice of 1 lemon and 1 orange
2 oz suet
1½ oz candied peel
1 oz grated almonds
1 tbspn brandy
1 tbspn rum
1 tspn spice

Method:
Put all except suet and currants through mincer then mix well together.

Lemonade

You need:
1 lemon
½ pint boiling water
4 lumps sugar

Method:
Remove the rind thinly from the lemon and squeeze out the juice.
Place the rind, juice and sugar in a jug and pour on the boiling
water. Cover until cold. Strain and serve.

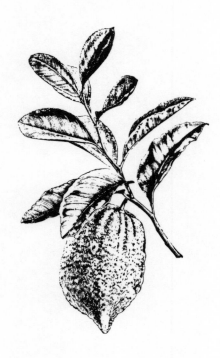